# This book belongs to

Carlson!

# Funny Facts about Animals

DERRYDALE BOOKS
NEW YORK

Written by Chee Yin Fun

Copyright © 1989 EPB Publishers Pte Ltd
Copyright © 1991 Ottenheimer Publishers, Inc.
This 1991 edition published by **DERRYDALE BOOKS,**
distributed by Outlet Book Company, Inc., a
Random House Company, 225 Park Avenue South,
New York, New York 10003.

All Rights Reserved
Printed and Bound in Singapore

ISBN 0-517-05663-1
8  7  6  5  4  3  2  1

## Hello Everybody!

I'm Max the Elephant and this is my good friend, Molly the Mouse. Together we are going to be your guides in this special book about animals. So be sure to stay with us.

## Happy Reading!

## The Laughing Jackass

The next time you hear a rude laugh, it may not be from a human but from a bird! The kookaburra, a forest kingfisher better known as the laughing jackass, has a most irritating call—it sounds like a very silly laugh.

# Let's Join the Band

**C**an you guess why a grey-feathered, Australian bird is called the trumpet-bird? Yes, it has a deep trumpet-like voice!

# The Whistling Hare

**A** hare that whistles? A tailless North American hare does just that! Its call is actually a very high-pitched whistle.

# Mating Call

**M**ost of the time, ostriches make only loud hissing noises. But, once the mating season begins, the males roar with the loudest, most booming voices you've ever heard.

# The Bird That Sews Its Own Nest

**F**irst, the Indian tailorbird finds two leaves close to each other. Using her beak, she pokes holes along the edges of the leaves before carefully sewing them together with plant fibers. This homemaker's cozy nest is ready once she furnishes it with feathers.

# Try Stroking It

The horned toad is actually a lizard with horns or spikes sticking out from its head and body! Despite its vicious appearance, the horned toad is really harmless. Just scratch or tickle its chin and you'll have a very happy pet.

# Extraordinary Beach Ball

**W**hen a puffer fish is taken out of the water, it opens a valve in its throat and swallows air. It then inflates to the size and shape of a beach ball! When you throw the fish back into the water, it closes its throat valve and deflates itself to its normal size and shape!

# If Fish Can Walk

**I**t's amazing, but there are some fish that can walk! The oriental climbing perch can leave the water and crawl onto land to look for food. Using its chest muscles and spiny gill covers, this fish can even climb tree roots. This is an unusual fish because it can survive out of the water!

# Not Crazy About Your Looks

The platypus, a resident of Australia, is a very strange-looking animal with a funny combination of features. It looks like a dog with no outer ears, its tail is flat, its front feet are webbed, and it has the bill of a duck!

# Sharpshooter

**T**he Siamese archer fish loves to eat insects that land on plants
hanging over shallow streams. Instead of waiting for the insects to
"drop" in on them, the fish catches its prey by "shooting" them down.
When the archer fish spots an insect, it takes aim with
its beaked snout and shoots "pellets" of water
at its victim. The insect, almost always
knocked off by the impact, tumbles
into the water to be gobbled up
by the fish.

## It's A Bird!
## It's A Plane!
## It's...It's A Snake?

**A**t first glance it looks like a long piece of ribbon floating in the air. But when you look closely, it is actually a very flat snake gliding through the air from tree to tree! The paradise tree snake, found in Asia, flattens its ribs, and using its body like a parachute, glides through the air.

## Let's Go A-Gliding

**H**as anyone ever heard of a frog that can glide through the air? There is one in Borneo! It rests in trees and has long toes with webs in between. The webs act like wings and hold the frog up in the air.

## Terrific Trunks

**D**o you know that an elephant's trunk is more than just a nose? It's like an extra arm. It's strong enough to lift a huge tree trunk and gentle enough to pick up a small peanut!

## Who's Afraid of a Mouse?

**M**any people think a mouse can scare an elephant silly! It's just not true. Can you imagine a little mouse frightening a huge elephant?

# What! No Brains?

**T**he most fascinating thing about the gecko, a type of house lizard, is that there is nothing at all between its ears. And I really mean nothing! If you were small enough, you could look in one ear and see right through to the other!

# I'm Not Dust, I'm A Bug!

The midge, the smallest insect in the world, is often mistaken for a speck of dust. It is so small that several midges fit on the head of a large push pin.

## Revealing Tails

When a dog wags its tail, it means that it is happy. But when a cat shakes its tail from side to side, WATCH OUT! It means that the cat is angry!

## Tell-Tail

**D**o you know that when a giraffe swishes its tail, it is actually sending a message to another giraffe? Giraffes are often said to have no voices, but they can produce a variety of sounds. This is very rare, however, because it's hard for them to make noises. So, they mainly communicate by moving their tails!

# They Sleep Standing Up

**B**elieve it or not, elephants can sleep on their feet! They can lie down and sleep, too. Generally, elephants sleep only about two to four hours a night—and they spend up to fifteen or eighteen hours just eating! No wonder they're so big!

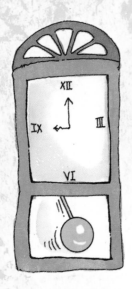

# Perfect Noses

**C**an you imagine drinking through your nose? Well, the elephant's trunk is its nose, so it certainly doesn't drink through it! The elephant sucks up a bucketful of water and squirts it into its mouth!

# That'll Show You

**R**elative to their sizes, an ant's brain takes up more of its body space than an elephant's brain!

## Enticing Music

If you're a male spider and want to attract a female, what should you do? Strum the strands of her web, of course!

# Have Eyes Will Travel

**F**latfish have bodies that are flat like a pancake. They lie and swim on one side with both their eyes on top. After each flatfish is born, one of its eyes actually travels across the top of its head to meet the other!

## Crazy Colors

**T**he octopus changes the color of its body whenever it becomes excited. What is so remarkable is that the octopus can turn different parts of its body into different colors at the same time!

# When Is An Insect A Stick?

**W**hen it is disguised as one! The stick insect looks like a twig so it is not easily detected by its enemies. It moves around very slowly and jerkily, and can remain motionless for hours.

# Hear Ye, Hear Ye!

**T**he grasshopper has ears but you'd have to search carefully to see them because they're located on unlikely parts of its body! Some grasshoppers have "ears" on their abdomens and at the base of their hind legs. Others have "ears" located on their first pair of legs!

# The Smartest Animal

**W**hen it comes to animals, the lovable chimpanzee tops the list in intelligence.

Research shows that chimps communicate by touching, and express their feelings by using a wide range of vocal sounds. They can even solve problems using logical reasoning.

# Grazing Galore

A goat will eat almost any plant. It will even eat the roots! So be careful! If you let a goat run free in your yard, you might not have one anymore!

# Fat in the Hump

**B**efore it begins a journey, a camel eats and drinks a lot. It eats so much that a hump of fat rises on its back. The camel's hump is actually a storage place for fat, which the camel's body uses during the journey. At the end of the journey, the hump will have shrunk in size.

# Eye-Opener

**T**he snake is unable to close its eyes or even blink them. During its long hibernation, a snake's eyes remain wide open.

# Balloon To The Rescue

The Chuckwalla, which lives in the desert, is a very remarkable lizard. Whenever danger approaches, the lizard will wriggle in between rocks and blow up its body like a balloon. This way, its body is wedged so tightly between the rocks, its enemy cannot pull it loose. When the enemy gives up and leaves, the Chuckwalla lets the air out and runs away.

# As Lazy As A Sloth

**B**e sure that no one ever calls you a sloth. The sloth is an extremely lazy South American mammal that sleeps hanging upside down on branches and moves around very slowly. It is certainly not a compliment to be compared to it!

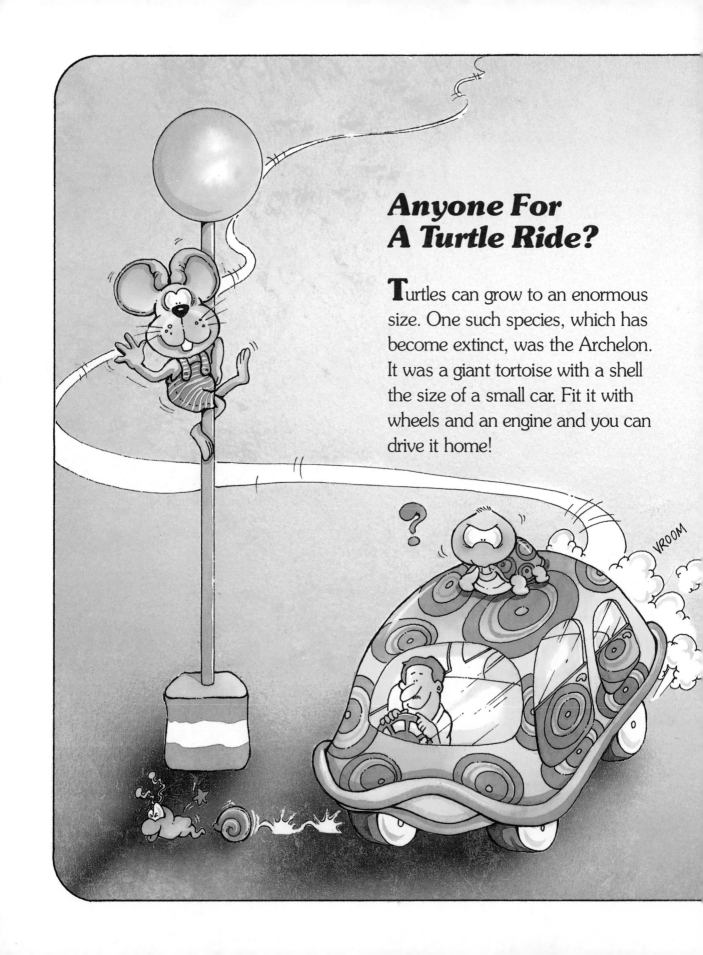

## Anyone For A Turtle Ride?

**T**urtles can grow to an enormous size. One such species, which has become extinct, was the Archelon. It was a giant tortoise with a shell the size of a small car. Fit it with wheels and an engine and you can drive it home!

VROOM

## A Fishy Situation

**F**ish live in the water and when they are pulled out, most of them wriggle around! This is because they breathe oxygen their gills absorb from the water. They can't breathe air when they're on land!

## A Tail Worth Digesting

**T**he Gila Monster, a poisonous lizard of the southwest, stores food in its fat tail, in case it can't find food anywhere else later!

# A Letter To My Love

**D**uring courtship, the Australian lyre bird sends out love messages with its beautiful tail!

# Telling Her Eggs By Their Taste

**A** female lizard can tell her own eggs by their taste. All she has to do is lick the eggs to be sure they are hers.

# How Does A Fly Catch Its Food?

**B**y spitting out saliva through its nose! Once the "food" is caught, the fly's saliva is then promptly sucked up again.